THE **DK** POCKET GUIDE TO

GOLF

PRACTICE DRILLS

THE DK POCKET GUIDE TO
GOLF
PRACTICE DRILLS

PETER BALLINGALL

PHOTOGRAPHY BY
STEVEN BARTHOLOMEW

DORLING KINDERSLEY
LONDON • NEW YORK • STUTTGART • MOSCOW

A Dorling Kindersley Book

MANAGING EDITOR Francis Ritter
MANAGING ART EDITOR Gillian Allan
US EDITOR Jill Hamilton

Produced for Dorling Kindersley by
Bob Gordon Design and Spider Books, London

First American Edition, 1995
2 4 6 8 10 9 7 5 3 1

Published in the United States by
Dorling Kindersley Publishing, Inc.
95 Madison Avenue
New York, New York 10016

Published in Great Britain by Dorling Kindersley Limited.
Distributed by Houghton Mifflin Company, Boston.

ISBN 0-7894-0193-2

Reproduced by Euroscan
Printed and bound in Great Britain by BPC Hazell Books Ltd

FOREWORD

There have been many teachers throughout the history of golf but there have been very few great teachers. Peter Ballingall is one of that rare breed because he is one of the game's great communicators. His approach to teaching is both simple and straightforward but, much more importantly, it works because of his rare gift of easy communication.

In this unique and stylish volume Peter has gathered together sound advice on good golfing methods and a collection of practice drills that are both invaluable and instantly accessible. I thoroughly commend it to you. It will never be far from my side.

MALCOLM CAMPBELL
GOLF MONTHLY

CONTENTS

HOW TO USE THIS BOOK

This book is organized so that it is easy to find the information you want. The book is arranged in three parts: the basic techniques of good golf; 33 practice drills; and sound advice on how to progress. The practice drills are grouped by type of shot (putting, chipping, pitching, full swing, and bunker). Each drill follows a simple format, which is explained on these pages.

LEFT RUNNING HEAD
Shows you which section you have turned to – here, the main section on practice drills and the subsection on putting.

PROBLEM
Helps you spot areas for improvement by pinpointing a difficulty and explaining how it affects play.

DRILL
Gives simple instructions on how to perform a drill that will solve the particular golfing problem described.

FEEL
Focuses on how it feels to play the shot correctly, giving you the confidence to know when you have done well.

BENEFIT
Explains clearly how the drill tackles your problem, and describes the benefit it brings to your game.

PUTTER HEAD DOWN

PROBLEM Do you hit the ball off-target and find that your stroke is not smooth? This is because your wrists are active during the stroke.

DRILL Hold out the putter in front of you, and bend the wrists so that the club head rises upward. Now lower the club head downward as far as it will go. Notice how the wrists have become arched. Adopt a putting stance, keeping the putter head down. Make some putts with the putter head down on both the backswing and throughswing.

Bend wrists and club head upward

FEEL The wrists feel as though they are in splints. They are no longer able to flick the putter head at the ball. The stroke seems to be made by the shoulders instead of the hands.

Stand ... with ... outstretch...

BENEFIT You learn to keep your wrists inactive so that your shoulders give the stroke a smoother rhythm and a sweeter contact with the ball for greater accuracy.

50

STEP-BY-STEP ILLUSTRATIONS
Clear and easy-to-follow photographs and artworks support the text and make the drills simple to practice.

KEY
Guide to visual devices used in this book.

Shows swing movement

Yellow balls are hit; orange not *Shows incorrect play* *Shows direction* *Shows body position*

IMPROVED RHYTHM AND CONTACT

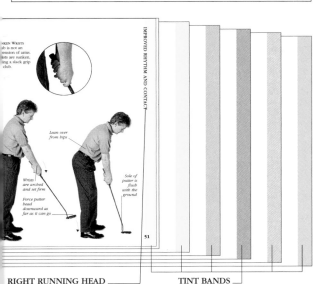

SUNKEN WRISTS
Club is not an extension of arms. Wrists are sunken, giving a slack grip on club.

Lean over from hips

Wrists are arched and set firm

Force putter head downward as far as it can go

Sole of putter is flush with the ground

51

RIGHT RUNNING HEAD
In the drills section, gives simple description of each drill's benefit. In sections one and three, gives spread title.

TINT BANDS
Pages are color coded for easy access. Colors are matched on the contents page and in the shirt color in each section.

9

INTRODUCTION

All aspiring golfers wish to have good ball control as well as a golf swing that really looks good. Wishing for these is one thing, but working hard to achieve them is another. You alone can do that. Finding a qualified teacher is a good start, but what matters is how you use your teacher's information to develop your own mastery of the game.

CONFIDENCE AND COMPETENCE

This book has two aims: to help you improve your technique and develop a "muscle memory" of how it feels to play a successful shot. Both are indispensable aspects of learning to play golf confidently and competently.

Too many tips serve only to confuse; everything included in this book has the single purpose of improving your actions into, and through the ball. To start with, I take you through the essentials of good golf – how to stand correctly, grip the club, transfer your weight, and find a sweet rhythm. Then I have selected 33 practice drills to help you improve your game.

HAPPIER AND MORE SUCCESSFUL GOLF

The drills are equally appropriate to the novice and the seasoned golfer. For the beginner they provide a foundation upon which to build; for the more experienced player they offer an opportunity to hone established skills. I hope that this book will lead you, whatever your level of experience, to happier and more successful golf.

PETER BALLINGALL

CHOOSING PRACTICE DRILLS

There are three reasons why you may play poor golf: confusion about what to do; doubts and uncertainties about the outcome; and misalignment in the address position. You may know what to do but don't believe it will happen this time; you may know what to do but set up inappropriately.

Either problem spoils your success. This gnaws at your self-assurance and leads to your doubting your ability. So you then try hard. This leads to tightness, which promotes errors and leads to further doubts next time around. These drills are designed to clear your mind and help you get off this carousel.

GOOD TECHNIQUE
All the drills help you develop control of the ball by helping you understand the essential geometry of club face alignment, swingpath, and plane.

THE PRACTICE DRILLS

This book contains a collection of 33 practice drills – simple but highly effective ways of improving your technique. Some have been in existence for a long time and are adapted from other teachers. Others I have devised myself in the course of my career as a professional teacher of the game.

OUT OF BALANCE
The drills teach you about balance, weight transfer, and the centrifugal forces that are found in all good swings.

SPLITTING WOOD
If you heave the club as though splitting wood, learn that power comes from an elasticity of movement that creates speed through impact.

FINDING A DRILL

The drills are grouped into different types of shot – putting, chipping, pitching, full swing, and bunker play. To start with, choose one area of your game on which to concentrate. Then look at the drills in your chosen section. Each works on a particular element of the shot. Choose one that focuses on your problem and that appeals to your imagination.

13

USING PRACTICE DRILLS

Resist the temptation to flit, butterfly-fashion,
between a large number of drills. Practice the
drills one at a time until you have mastered
each one. Understanding the aim of each
drill is important. So too is understanding
why it will help. A third crucial element
is to become fully aware of the feel of
your actions. Intellectualize (learn the
"how"); conceptualize (understand
the "why"); then react (experience
the "feeling").

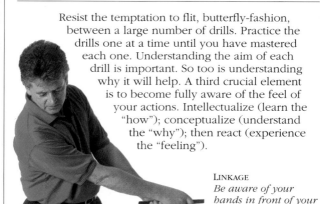

LINKAGE
*Be aware of your
hands in front of your
torso into, through,
and just after impact.*

UNDERSTANDING WHY
What your mind can
perceive your body can
achieve. Not until you
understand the "how"
and the "why" will your
game improve. The style
of your swing is quite
unimportant: control of
the ball is what counts.

EASY TURN
*Feel that you are turning
easily on the backswing as
though conserving energy.*

CREATE GOOD HABITS
Notice how your body feels as you
execute each drill. When you do
something different it feels strange
at first. Do not be nervous about
this. Hold a position as you perform
your drill and observe how it feels
so that you can recognize it next
time. Repetition of the good things
creates good habits.

SMOOTH MOVE
*A powerful swing
begins in the feet, so
feel that the arms
swing down at the
same time as you
transfer your weight.*

15

HOW TO PRACTICE

Practice does not make perfect: it makes permanent. So if you practice incorrectly you will be permanently wrong. Perfect practice makes perfect. Therefore, the key is to practice intelligently.

SHORT AND SWEET Short and frequent practice sessions are more beneficial than isolated, lengthy ones. If you apply yourself to one or two drills for five minutes a day, every day for a month, you will become expert at them. You will understand how they will transform your game and you will establish a lasting muscle memory. The movements will become habitual and will come through in your golf swing without the need for conscious thought.

SLOW MOTION Practice each drill in slow motion until you are confident of the moves and feel comfortable with them. Then build up your speed slowly until you are making successful shots at full speed.

BE PATIENT It takes a little time for new habits to become established. The rewards, however, are well worth the wait.

MIRROR, MIRROR
*Practice in front
of a full-length
mirror or glass
doors whenever
possible. It is
important to see
the movements you
are making so that
you can develop a
feel for the action.*

MENTAL PRACTICE

Every golfer admits that golf is played in the mind.
Opinions vary about the extent to which the mind affects
play. Some say that golf is 90 percent mental, others that it
is less so. All agree, however, that the mental aspects
of golf make up considerably more than half of the skills
necessary in order to play the game to a high level.

Understanding the technical skills is of little use without
appreciating how to improve the mental skills. Self-
improvement begins only when you recognize the powers
of concentration, visualization, and rational thought.

CONCENTRATION This is the art of focusing attention on
one thing to the exclusion of all else. As you perform your
drills, become absorbed in what you are doing and in how
it feels physically; that is, be "mindful," not "thoughtful."

VISUALIZATION Visualization is practiced by all good
golfers and forms the basis of your progress. It is the art
of putting onto your internal movie screen an image
that depicts and predicts success.

Visualizing a successful shot is easy when you ask this
question before playing any shot: "What do I want the
ball to do?" As you survey the target, your imagination
will create pictures of the ball flying through the air and
landing in the target zone. It will show you everything in
detail: the weight of the shot, the direction of flight, and
the roll of the ball.

The mind becomes peaceful and relaxed as it engages
with the target in this way and enables the brain to react
more confidently and competently. When practicing a
drill, use your imagination to "see" the effect it will have
on your performance. By seeing its value the brain will
send appropriate messages to the muscles and organs
of the body to accomplish that drill effectively.

RATIONAL THOUGHT

When progress seems slow it does not mean that you cannot succeed. It means, simply, that you must work harder to establish the new habits. If your golf is important to you, you will persevere.

IN PRACTICE Mental practice requires no club and no ball. The quantum leap from subconscious incompetence (blissful ignorance) through conscious competence (skill level increasing with thought) to subconscious competence (reacting naturally on a higher level) can be shortened. Simply create a scene in your mind and put yourself into it. You are performing the shot perfectly. Replay this mental "video" often.

CLEAR FOCUS
You can improve your play by fostering a positive mental attitude.

19

BASIC
TECHNIQUES

The first step to improving your golf technique is to have a sound understanding of the golf swing and a good set-up routine.

THE GOLF SWING

Everyone possesses a natural style of golf swing. History has taught that no two champions ever swung the club alike: individual style has played a role in their success. History has also taught, however, that all great players do something similar in, to, and through the hitting area. It is in this area of the golf swing that control of the ball is to be found.

Upper body and arms move back together

Body is comfortably positioned, ready for action

FLOWING ACTION The golf swing is essentially a flowing action of the arms, hands, and body interacting independently, but in synchronization with each other, from a semistationary start to a balanced finish. It is a rhythmical, "elastic" movement – not a series of contortions.

While the arms do swing the club, the powerhouse of the golf swing is the body. The energy is created through its rotations and the transfer of weight.

Once you are clear about how the simple geometry of swing will give you control of the ball, your actions from beginning to finish must be naturally coordinated. This can happen only when you stop trying too hard or thinking too much about what you are doing.

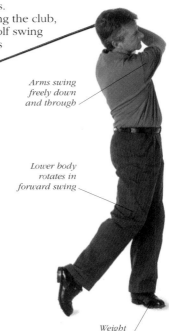

Arms swing freely down and through

Lower body rotates in forward swing

Weight transfers

PROPERTIES OF THE SWING

Understanding the properties of the swing is important to help you form the foundations of a good swing and therefore of a successful game.

THE PENDULUM Picture the pendulum of a grandfather clock swinging in a smooth, rhythmical, and unhurried way. It is suspended by a chain from a hub, or axis, in the clock face, forming a radius. This makes the pendulum move in the shape of an arc.

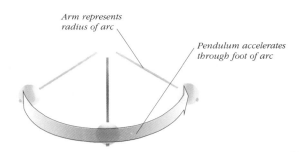

Arm represents radius of arc

Pendulum accelerates through foot of arc

When the pendulum swings from left to right, the beginning of the arc seems to begin at an easy pace and gather momentum through the foot of the arc. Then, the start of the arc from right to left once again starts at the same easy pace. The pendulum may swing either fast or slowly. The swing is natural and uninhibited: no external force is applied.

THE HUMAN PENDULUM Now translate this action to golf. The base of the neck is the hub, which remains still throughout the swing. The arms are the chain; they maintain a relatively wide radius as they swing the club freely from one side to the other.

The beginning of the forward swing of the club head starts at the same easy pace as the beginning of the backswing, although it accelerates through the foot of the arc. The swing is unhurried. There is no aggression or applied physical force.

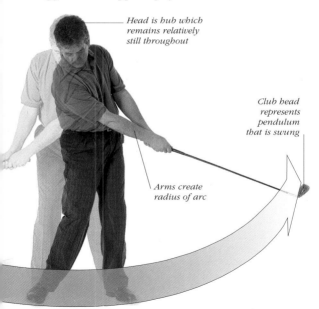

Head is hub which remains relatively still throughout

Club head represents pendulum that is swung

Arms create radius of arc

RHYTHM, TEMPO, AND TIMING

Rhythm, tempo, and timing are fundamentals of a good swing action.

RHYTHM Rhythm is a swing with a beat. In golf, the start of the downswing begins at the same pace as the start of the backswing.

REGULAR BEAT
Rhythm of your swing may be fast or slow – but it should be regular, as blue lines show.

Upper body turns as arm prepares to throw

Underhand throwing action demonstrates rhythm, tempo, and timing

Left arm balances body

Weight moves into right side

TEMPO Tempo refers to the speed of the swing. A golf swing can be fast or slow – either is satisfactory as long as it has a regular rhythm. Find a speed for your swing that suits you. Don't be frightened of experimenting.

MARKING TIME
Metronome marks regular beat at speed of your choosing.

Action is coordinated and balanced

Body turns to face target

Weight transfers

TIMING Timing describes how the movements of the body coordinate during the swing action. Movements of the hands and arms synchronize with those of the major muscle groups of the upper and lower body.

Perfect timing is perfect coordination. It occurs when the arms and hands swing the club down, to, and through the ball in time with the transfer of weight and turn of the body to the target.

27

CENTRIFUGAL FORCE

Centrifugal force is an energy that emanates outward directly from a rotational center. In almost every sport where something is thrown or hit with a bat, centrifugal forces are in action when power is required. The discus thrower, baseball pitcher, and tennis player all achieve their power through the transfer of weight and rotations of the major muscle groups of the body, which fuel the smaller muscles of the hands and arms.

THE POWER OF THE GOLF SWING In golf, distance is achieved when the club head travels in an arc that brushes with the ball-to-target line, and when its club face is square to that swingpath through impact. For the club head to travel at optimum speed through this point, the force comes not from the hands or arms but from the turns of the body.

Upper body turns as arms swing racket back

Weight moves onto right foot

Upper body turns to coil body like a spring

Picture skaters on a rink, arms linked to form a chain. The skater on the outside moves faster than he could skate solo, propelled by the energy emanating from the person in the center, who simply turns on the spot.

Hips and midriff rotate

Left heel comes off ground as weight moves onto right foot

Right knee moves around toward target

So it is with the club face. It responds to the energies emanating from the feet, up through the body as it turns, and down through the arms, and into the club shaft. This creates top speed, and thus power, distance, and control.

Feet transfer weight and right foot ends on toe with heel pointing to rear

29

WEIGHT TRANSFER

Balance is fundamental to an efficient and consistent golf swing. So too is weight transfer. As long as your golf swing is contained within the balance of your stance you can achieve both good transfer of weight and power from your swing.

ADDRESS
Feet, knees, hips, and shoulders all support each other at address.

BALANCE POINTS

The point of balance moves into the right side on the backswing, and then into the left during the throughswing. The joints in the body that give balance are the feet, knees, hips, and shoulders. These parts of the body must always support each other – at address, on the backswing, and at the end of the throughswing.

EQUAL SCALES
For medium irons, weight is distributed equally at address.

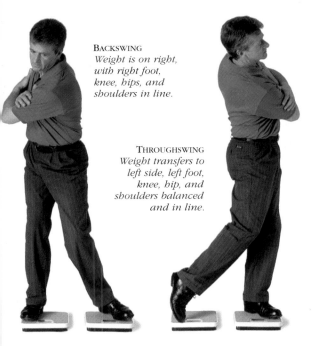

BACKSWING
Weight is on right, with right foot, knee, hips, and shoulders in line.

THROUGHSWING
Weight transfers to left side, left foot, knee, hip, and shoulders balanced and in line.

WEIGHTED RIGHT
Majority of body weight is on right side on backswing.

WEIGHTED LEFT
Left foot, knee, and hip take most of weight at finish.

THE SET-UP

The set-up at address is crucial to good, consistent play. Golf has been described as 98 percent set-up and 2 percent start. It is important to be clear in your mind about the techniques of playing a shot. It is also vital that you believe you can succeed. But neither of these elements will ensure your success if you set up inappropriately at the beginning.

Grip, alignment, stance, and posture – GASP – are the fundamental aspects of good set-up. They are described in detail on the following pages.

RELEVANCE OF GOOD SET-UP When practicing or playing golf you are literally setting everything up for a reaction to take place. You have selected your target and chosen a club. You should have a clear mental vision of how the ball is going to fly and roll. You have subconsciously, or consciously, gathered information on wind conditions, the lie of the ball, and the contours of the fairway or the speed of the green. All these elements have been taken in through your senses. Once you have assimilated this information you simply move into position and react to it.

Every part of you that is above the line of the shaft at address should feel passive: hands, arms, stomach, shoulders, and facial muscles. Everything below that line should feel springy: feet, knees, and legs. Pay attention to feeling this way.

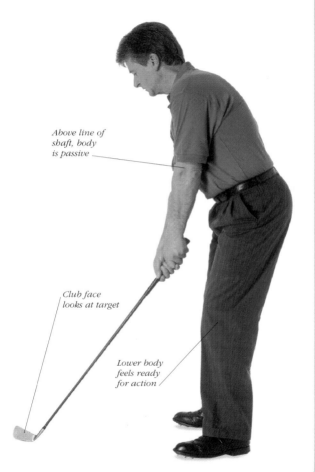

*Above line of
shaft, body
is passive*

*Club face
looks at target*

*Lower body
feels ready
for action*

GRIP

The single purpose of the golf swing is to present the club face squarely to the target at, and through, impact. The hands connect the club face to the power source of the golf swing action. The world's greatest players agree that the hands control the club face and that their grip gives them control of the ball.

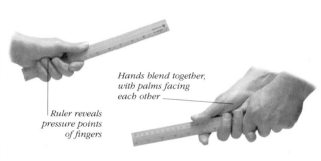

Hands blend together, with palms facing each other

Ruler reveals pressure points of fingers

HOLDING THE CLUB The palms must face each other on the grip in order to act as one unit. They must blend together and with the grip in a light but secure way so that they naturally deliver the club face squarely to the target at impact every time.

Taking hold of a ruler will teach you about the pressure points of the fingers. Feel those same pressure points as you take hold of the club. Avoid holding the grip tightly: tension will transmit through your arms and shoulders, making a free swing impossible to achieve.

VARDON GRIP
Smallest finger of right hand overlaps second finger of left hand underneath.

INTERLOCKING GRIP
Smallest finger of right hand interlocks with index finger of left hand.

BASEBALL GRIP
Hands are placed right below left on grip.

ADAPTING THE GRIP You may adapt your grip, using the Vardon, interlocking, or baseball method, to suit your individual style of play. Find the best style for you.

An old golfing adage says, "If the ball bends to the left, move both hands to the left on the grip. If the ball bends to the right, move both hands to the right." This adjustment resets the club face alignment at impact and the direction of its swingpath through the ball.

HAND POSITION
V-shape of right hand points to right ear. V-shape of left hand points to right shoulder.

ALIGNMENT

Club face alignment and body alignment at address are fundamental to attaining control of the ball. The ball always ends up in the direction in which the club face was looking at impact, so align it squarely to the target at the start. The swingpath of the club head is determined by the alignment of the shoulders, hips, knees, and feet, so align them parallel with the ball-to-target line at address for the ball to fly straight.

TAKING GOOD AIM

Aiming yourself toward the target is the one thing *not* to do if you wish the ball to fly straight to your target. Imagine that you are standing on one line of a railroad track with the ball in front of you on the other track. The club face looks directly down the track that runs to the target. Although it appears that the railroad lines meet on the horizon, they do not: they remain parallel to one another.

SQUARE STANCE
Club face points to target with body parallel to target line.

Align your stance parallel with the target but to the left of it. Remember that the arc of the swing brushes with the ball-to-target line on a tangent "inside-square-to-inside" (see page 90). If the swingpath crosses the target line from either the inside or the outside, the ball will not go to the target. This geometry is useful when you wish to correct a fault or to hit the ball with intentional "draw" or "fade," altering the ball's line of flight.

CLOSED STANCE
Club face is square with body aligned to right for hook.

OPEN STANCE
Club face is square with body aligned to left for slice.

STANCE AND BALL POSITION

The design of the club determines where the ball sits in relation to your feet at address. Here is a simple way of getting it right every time.

HOLD IT, AIM IT, FACE IT First, take hold of the club with your arms extended in front of you. Second, keeping both hands on the grip, lean over with your right foot forward to place and aim the club face behind the ball.

HOLD IT
Hold out arms in front of you to check club face alignment.

Third, keeping both hands on the grip and the club in position, align feet, knees, hips, and shoulders parallel to the ball-to-target line. For all clubs, the feet remain a comfortable shoulder-width apart for perfect balance.

This routine has two benefits: you will find a self-regulated distance to stand from the ball with any club; the ball will find its own position relative to your feet.

RELATIVE PLACEMENT
For driver, ball is near left heel; for mid-iron, between center of stance and left heel; for lofted iron, it is in center of stance.

AIM IT
Lean over from hips and onto right foot to align club face square to target.

FACE IT
Align body parallel to ball-to-target line without moving club.

POSTURE

Good posture is essential. The plane of the swing, the direction of the swingpath, and alignment at impact are all influenced by the way you stand at the start.

The ideal posture is of straight lines and angles. Lean over from the hips – never the waist. This keeps the lower spine straight, letting the hands and arms hang down freely below the chin. It also promotes balance – an important requirement. When the lower spine is straight, the body can turn easily both ways without changing the angle of tilt of the spine, and therefore the swingplane.

SIDE TO SIDE
Gap between heels is hip-width, giving sideways balance.

FRONT TO BACK
Head in front balances bottom out behind.

UP AND DOWN
Weight is supported from hips down, creating balance.

THREE-DIMENSIONAL BALANCE

Placing the feet a comfortable width
apart creates balance from side to
side. Leaning the head over
(but with the chin up)
counterbalances the
bottom, which sticks out
a little, creating balance
from front to back. The
bulk of the body weight is
supported by the feet, knees,
and hips, creating balance up
and down. Never do anything
in your golf swing that will
interfere with this balance.

The posture alters slightly as
you change from the driver to a
wedge. You stand a little taller
for the driver and are more over
the ball for a wedge. Yet the
principles of balance remain.

UNIVERSAL PRINCIPLES
*Principles of balance
remain whatever club
you are using.*

HEAD POSITION

"Keep your head down, and keep it still," is possibly the most misunderstood command in golf. The thing to do is to keep your chin *up*. How can you make a full turn for a powerful swing when your chin is buried on your chest? The ideal head position is attained when raising your eyes without lifting your head lets you see the horizon, and lowering your eyes lets you see the ball.

On putts, chips, and all other shots that do not require power, the head must remain still throughout the stroke. On all full golf swings, the head must be allowed to move. It rotates a little on the backswing and throughswing; moves slightly to the right as the upper body coils; and moves back as the weight transfers into the impact area. But it must move neither ahead of the ball before contact is made nor up and down. Try the exercise illustrated here.

Amateurs try hard to keep their head still on the power shots, thereby stifling all natural mobility. They then allow the head to wiggle loosely on the short shots that need accuracy.

FACING FRONT
Make mark on mirror so that reflection is opposite your throat.

RIGHT TURN
*When turning to right,
mark is reflected
against back of neck.*

LEFT TURN
*Mark shows against
back of neck in swing
to other side.*

43

PRACTICE
DRILLS

*The second step to good golf is to
understand which areas of your
game need improvement and to
work on them single-mindedly.*

PUTTING DRILLS

Putting has often been referred to as a science all on its own. Over the ages, golfers have developed different ways of holding the club and have created putters of every possible design.

Conventional right hand below left method

Broom handle method

The putting stroke is a pendulum action where the movement of the club head is created by a gentle rocking of the shoulders (see pages 24–5). The hands lead the club face through the ball; the club face "collects" the ball rather than hits it. Putting is easiest when the hands and wrists do nothing.

There are several methods used by great players to eliminate the wristy flick: the conventional right hand below left; the broom handle; the left hand below right; the Langer; and the conventional "reverse overlap," with the left forefinger pressing against the fingers of the right hand. Experiment until you find a method that suits you.

The putting drills will help you control the club and ball; eliminate use of the wrists; and synchronize the movements between arms, shoulders, and hands to produce a sound, repetitive action. Also vitally important is the need to believe that your putts will go in.

Left hand below right method

Langer method

Conventional "reverse overlap" method

FINGER PRESS

PROBLEM Do you have difficulty gauging the distance to the target and miss your putts to the left of the hole? If so, you are flicking the putter head at the ball with your wrists.

DRILL Hold the putter with the left forefinger overlapping the third finger of the right hand. Address the ball, pressing the left forefinger against the fingers of the right hand. Notice how the putter head moves backward a little. Make sure that the hands sit over the ball. Maintain the pressure as you make your stroke. The right wrist maintains its position throughout.

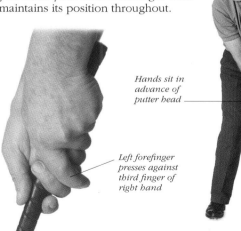

Hands sit in advance of putter head

Left forefinger presses against third finger of right hand

FEEL The action feels more compact. The back of the left hand seems to lead the putter head. You feel that the ball is collected by the putter – there is no sensation of hit.

BENEFIT The club face looks squarely to the target through impact, which improves accuracy. You have more control of the roll of the ball.

Pressing forefinger makes club head move backward

Hands remain in advance of putter head through impact

49

PUTTER HEAD DOWN

PROBLEM Do you hit the ball off-target and find that your stroke is not smooth? This is because your wrists are active during the stroke.

DRILL Hold out the putter in front of you, and bend the wrists so that the club head rises upward. Now lower the club head downward as far as it will go. Notice how the wrists have become arched. Adopt a putting stance, keeping the putter head down. Make some putts with the putter head down on both the backswing and throughswing.

FEEL The wrists feel as though they are in splints. They are no longer able to flick the putter head at the ball. The stroke seems to be made by the shoulders instead of the hands.

BENEFIT You learn to keep your wrists inactive so that your shoulders give the stroke a smoother rhythm and a sweeter contact with the ball for greater accuracy.

Bend wrists and club head upward

Stand tall with arms outstretched

SUNKEN WRISTS
Club is not an extension of arms. Wrists are sunken, giving a slack grip on club.

Lean over from hips

Wrists are arched and set firm

Force putter head downward as far as it can go

Sole of putter is flush with the ground

BOOK DRILL

PROBLEM Do you slice your putts, leaving them short and to the right of the hole, or pulled to the left? Your arms, shoulders, and wrists may be out of synchronization, causing you to lift the putter in the takeaway and swing it off line.

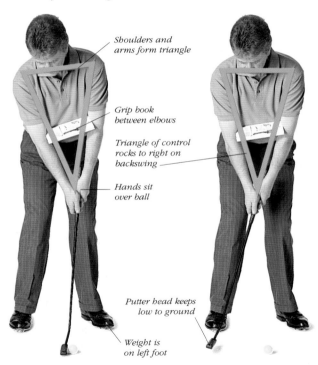

Shoulders and arms form triangle

Grip book between elbows

Triangle of control rocks to right on backswing

Hands sit over ball

Putter head keeps low to ground

Weight is on left foot

DRILL Support a medium-sized book between your elbows. Make your stroke without letting the book slip. If you practice in front of a mirror you will see how the shoulders and arms move as one, creating a triangle of control.

Triangle of control rocks to left as stroke is made

Firm wrists lead club head

Putter head collects ball on upswing

FEEL The stroke feels compact and secure. You feel a gentle rocking movement of the shoulders.

BENEFIT Gripping a book helps establish a sense of your arms, shoulders, and wrists moving as one unit. This moves the club head through a shallow arc, creating topspin and a more accurate roll to the target.

ONE-THIRD: TWO-THIRDS

PROBLEM Do your putts end up either longer or shorter than you intended? This may be because your backswing is too large. This slows the club head through impact, which makes it difficult to gauge the pace of the putt.

DRILL Place a ball opposite the right foot and another one (the object ball) just inside the left heel. Place the club head between the balls and play the object ball without touching the other one.

FEEL You feel the shoulders rock a small way back and a longer way through the stroke. The smooth rhythm of the rocking action makes the club head seem to collect the ball as it passes.

BENEFIT By giving the stroke a one-third: two-thirds ratio – taking the club head one-third back on the backswing and two-thirds forward on the throughswing – the club head accelerates through impact. This gives the putt the correct pace to take the ball to target.

Weight favors left side

Take up position to play yellow ball

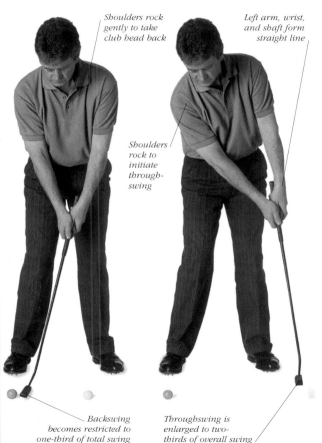

Shoulders rock gently to take club head back

Left arm, wrist, and shaft form straight line

Shoulders rock to initiate through-swing

Backswing becomes restricted to one-third of total swing

Throughswing is enlarged to two-thirds of overall swing

TWO-CLUB CHANNEL

PROBLEM Do you miss putts when you are sure you are reading the line to target accurately? This could be caused by a poor swingpath through impact.

DRILL Place two clubs on the ground to form a channel only slightly wider than the width of the putter head, and pointing to the target. Place a ball between the clubs and make the putt, ensuring that the club head moves through the ball and along the channel.

FEEL On short putts you feel the putter move straight back from the ball. On longer ones the head tracks on a more obvious arc, but still within the channel. Feel the left shoulder lead the putter to the target.

BENEFIT You learn to allow the putter to track on a slight arc inside the ball-to-target line on the backswing and then straight through to the target on the forward swing. This gives you greater accuracy.

Stand tall, leaning over from hips, with eyes over ball

End of club is opposite right foot

Channel is slightly wider than putter head

EXTENDED BACKSWING
A backswing that is too long would extend beyond channel.

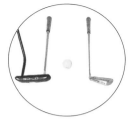

Short backswing is contained within channel

Club head tracks marginally inside on backswing

Swingpath of putter goes down channel directly toward target

MIRROR DRILL

PROBLEM Anxiety about holing or missing a putt often results in the eyes and head coming up too early, in order to see what has happened. This drags the ball off line as the shoulders pull the club to the left.

DRILL Place a ball on top of a small mirror. Take up the address position so that you see the reflection of your eyes in the mirror. Notice that your eyes sit parallel with the top and bottom edges of the mirror; this means that your shoulders are parallel with the ball-to-target line. Make your putting stroke. Keep looking at the reflection of your eyes until long after the ball has gone.

FEEL You feel the right shoulder move more under the chin than around it. The left arm, hand, and putter seem to separate from the left side of the body as the club moves directly toward the target.

Take up address with ball on top of mirror

Head remains
motionless
throughout
stroke

BENEFIT Focusing your
eyes on the mirror
keeps your body facing
the ball-to-target line
throughout the shot.
This gives you a correct
swingpath and sends
the ball to the target.

Eyes are parallel
with top and bottom
edges of mirror

Eyes still look
at mirror after
ball has gone

Club face has
collected ball

EYES CLOSED

PROBLEM Do you try too hard to get things right? The eyes often play tricks on you and affect your stroke if you do not also use other senses in playing a shot.

DRILL With your eyes open, assess where the hole is and how much of an action will be needed to make the ball reach the hole. Then close your eyes and make the stroke.

Before opening your eyes, assess where the ball has finished in relation to the target. You may be wildly inaccurate at first but in a short time you will amaze yourself with your accuracy.

FEEL Your feel for pace and the rhythm of your action becomes more acute. Your mind becomes peacefully focused as it experiences the flow of the movement.

BENEFIT When the eyes are closed, other senses come into play and your awareness increases with your feedback of feel. This results in greater relaxation and accuracy.

Take up address position in line with target

With eyes closed, simply react to target

Backswing feels smooth and unhurried

Throughswing is unhurried as you remain focused on target

CHIPPING DRILLS

Even great players miss the green on occasion – but all can chip the ball close to the hole when they do. This removes the pressure from your long game and allows good scores. The object of the chip shot is to fly the ball through the air to the nearest flat surface

Shoulders sit parallel with intended line of flight

Hands are ahead of club head and over ball

Weight is firmly on left foot

Club head moves through ball, facing target

of the putting green and allow the ball to roll, like a putt, upon landing.

Aim to move the club through the ball as though sending it forward, not upward. Make no attempt to get the club head under the ball. Keep the hands in advance of the club head through impact to enable the loft of the club to deflect the ball upward and forward. Only a small swing is needed to propel the ball to the nearest flat surface. The ball rolls a little with a lofted club, farther with a less lofted one.

Hands lead club head into and through ball

Stance may be slightly open to target line

Weight favors forward foot

63

BUTT OF GRIP TO WRIST

PROBLEM When chipping, does the ball shoot along the ground a long way past the hole? If so, this is because you are trying to scoop the club face under the ball with the wrists to get it airborne, and in doing so contact the ball on the upswing.

DRILL Secure the end of the grip to the left wrist using a wrist band. Make the shot, keeping the grip snug into the wrist. Brush the grass as you swing through.

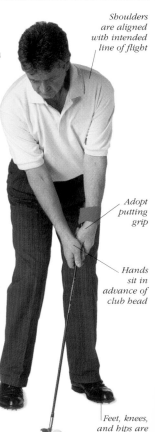

Shoulders are aligned with intended line of flight

Adopt putting grip

Hands sit in advance of club head

Feet, knees, and hips are slightly open

Tuck butt of grip into wrist band

Hold club farther down shaft than usual

FEEL The left arm draws the club away on the backswing, keeping the club head near the ground. The forward swing begins with weight transfer to the left; the right knee folds in toward the target; the hips open to allow the arms, hands, and club head to pass through the ball.

Arms retain triangle with shoulders

Butt of grip is still snug against wrist

Back of wrist leads club head

BENEFIT The arms and hands go through the ball ahead of the club head and the ball rises of its own accord as the club face passes through it. This results in flying chip shots.

Right knee folds inward to target

Club head has collected ball

TWO AT ONCE

PROBLEM Do you stub the ground in front of the ball when chipping? A wristy flick is usually to blame, catching the ball on the upswing and skimming it across the green to the rough on the other side.

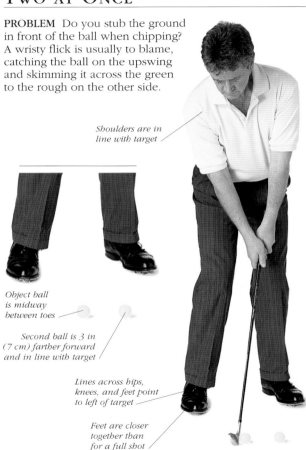

Shoulders are in line with target

Object ball is midway between toes

Second ball is 3 in (7 cm) farther forward and in line with target

Lines across hips, knees, and feet point to left of target

Feet are closer together than for a full shot

DRILL Adopt the usual stance, with the object ball opposite your nose, and your eyes parallel to the ball-to-target line. The ball appears to be in the middle of the stance. Place another ball about 3 in (7 cm) to the left of the first ball, in line with the target. Focus on contacting both balls with one swing. Once you have hit the first ball, continue your swing to hit the second one. The first will be on its way.

FEEL The swing feels longer and shallower than before. The arms seem to separate from the body and extend toward the target. The club head lags behind the hands, staying low through the ball.

BENEFIT By extending your swing you will make pure, crisp contact with the ball, which will fly through the air toward the target.

Hips turn, right knee folds toward target, right heel comes out of ground

First ball flies over second ball, toward target

PUTT IT

PROBLEM Do you find it difficult to stop flicking your wrists? When this happens, your club scuffs the ground or clips the ball on the upswing.

DRILL Using a No. 7 or 8 iron, set up as for putting, with your body aligned with the ball-to-target line. Hold the club down the grip, using the putting

Shoulders, hips, knees, and feet are parallel with ball-to-target line

Hold club down grip to approximate length of your putter

Club face is slightly open

Heel of club is off ground

Club head sits on its toe

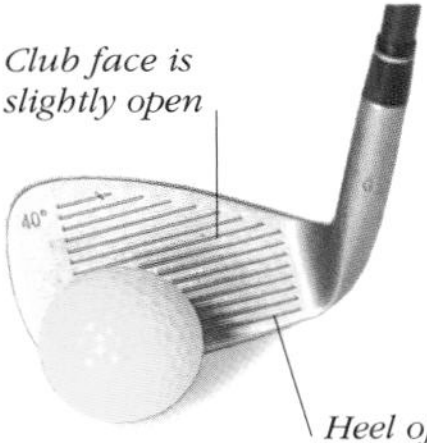

grip (see pages 46–7). Arch the wrists so that the club head sits on its toe. Place the ball inside the left heel and open the club face slightly. Putt through the ball, rocking the shoulders gently. Aim to move the ball forward, not upward.

In putting through ball, hands remain in advance of club head

FEEL The hands feel as if they only connect the club face to the shoulders, which activate the rocking movement. You feel as if the club head is collecting the ball rather than hitting it.

BENEFIT If you consider the shot as nothing more than putting with a lofted putter you will cure your wristy flick and make good chip shots.

THE PRO'S APPROACH

PROBLEM Do you prefer to chip with your favorite wedge or other lofted club in every situation but find it hard to control the flight and pace on the ball when rolling it across the green?

DRILL Adopt a slightly open stance but with the shoulders aligned with your intended line of flight and the body weight favoring the left side. Place the ball farther back in the stance

Feet, knees, and hips are aligned slightly to left of target

Weight favors left side

Club moves back, with head close to ground

Position ball farther back in stance than usual

than usual. Play the shot mainly with the arms, so that the toe of the club overtakes the heel through impact, creating topspin.

FEEL The right forearm rotates over the left. The movement is smooth and unhurried. There is a mild inflection of the wrists, although they are only reacting rather than playing a major role.

BENEFIT Rolling the right wrist over the left makes it passive. This results in the ball flying low and rolling farther, as though you were using a less lofted club.

Right forearm overtakes left

Arc of swing is shallow as toe overtakes heel

PITCHING DRILLS

The essence of the pitch shot is to fly the ball high through the air and land it on the green with the minimum of roll. To achieve backspin on the ball so that it stops quickly requires a crisp downward swing of the arms, with the hands leading the club head. The aim is to hit first the ball – then the turf.

To attain this, the body weight must be firmly on the left side at impact. To make the ball fly high, swing the club down, keeping the right hand inactive. The club head

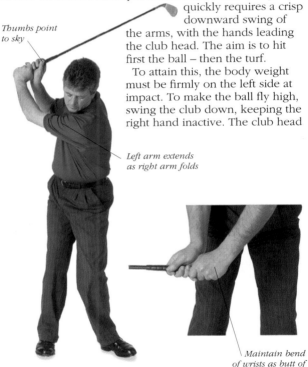

Thumbs point to sky

Left arm extends as right arm folds

Maintain bend of wrists as butt of grip pulls down

lags behind the hands. Transfer weight in unison with the swing of the arms, and let the club do the rest. Swing the club head through the ball as though it were not there. The feet, knees, and hips play their part to initiate the forward swing, although on shorter shots of 40–50 yds (40–50 m) their contribution is small.

Hands lead club head into and through ball

Body turns to target at throughswing

Midriff turns to target as arms swing club down

Weight transfers to left side

UMBRELLA SWING

PROBLEM Do you have difficulty in hitting high wedge shots from 60–80 yds (60–80 m) out? Do you "thin" the ball or hit the ground in front of it? If so, your swingplane is probably too flat.

DRILL Place an umbrella in the ground about 3 ft (1 m) out from your right heel. Make your backswing without knocking over the umbrella. Set the club face and bend the wrists early to avoid contact. Turn your shoulders at the same time. Now position the umbrella to the side of your left foot and make some shots without knocking it over.

Toe of club points to sky

Bend wrists early

Position umbrella in line with right heel

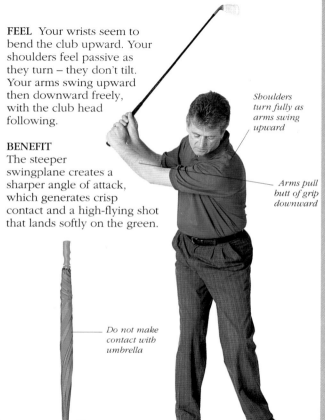

FEEL Your wrists seem to bend the club upward. Your shoulders feel passive as they turn – they don't tilt. Your arms swing upward then downward freely, with the club head following.

BENEFIT
The steeper swingplane creates a sharper angle of attack, which generates crisp contact and a high-flying shot that lands softly on the green.

Shoulders turn fully as arms swing upward

Arms pull butt of grip downward

Do not make contact with umbrella

TOWEL DRILL

PROBLEM Missing the green from within 50 yds (50 m) damages morale and is costly in terms of your score. The prime cause is poor timing – the arms, legs, and body are out of synchronization.

DRILL Place a towel across your chest and make your swing without letting it slip. As the distance in this instance is quite short, a half swing will suffice. The shoulders turn on the backswing at the same time as the wrists bend and the arms swing upward. The body weight shifts a little toward the right side.

As the arms swing down, the weight transfers to the left and the midriff rotates to face the target.

FEEL The towel, kept in place by your upper arms, gives you a feeling of confinement. Your arms feel connected to your upper body. Your feet play a much greater role, and they, together with your midriff, fuel the action.

Upper body turns as arms swing upward

Hands are opposite torso

Grip towel comfortably with upper arms

Weight moves toward right side

BENEFIT Purposefully keeping your arms close to your body by wrapping a towel around your chest in this way teaches you to synchronize the movements of your arms, legs, and body – or the towel would slip. This allows you to gain both a more authoritative strike and a crispness of contact with the ball.

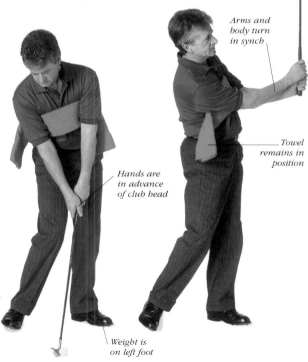

Arms and body turn in synch

Towel remains in position

Hands are in advance of club head

Weight is on left foot

77

FULL SWING DRILLS

All the drills explained in this section are devised to improve your swingpath into and through the ball on an arc that travels "inside-square-to-inside" the ball-to-target line (see page 90). The drills also help you recognize and establish a good plane of swing, correct hand action, and power.

Upper body turns fully

Hips turn only a little

Hips rotate

Hands are opposite torso

Weight is on right side

Weight moves in to left side

78

The drills center around the four basic
positions that are important in golf:
the address position; the top of the
backswing; the impact position; and the
finish. They are grouped in such a way
that drills tackling a particular element
of the swing are placed together:
those that improve hand
action; drills to correct
swingplane; and drills
to encourage better
body position.

*Torso looks
to left*

*Body is
perfectly
balanced
at finish*

*Belt
buckle
faces
target*

What is equally important to
learn is that the whole
swing action is greater than
the sum of its parts. Good
shots won't come until you
allow your club head to
swing through the ball to
a full and balanced finish.

*Right heel is off ground
and looking to rear*

*Weight is
fully on left foot*

HAND ACTION

PROBLEM Errant shots are the result of the club face being either closed or open to the target at impact. This is caused by ignorance of how the hands should bend in the golf swing.

Toe and scorelines of club are looking skyward

Right wrist bends back on itself and left wrist rotates a little when club reaches hip height

DRILL Hold the club as described on pages 34–5, with the hands blending together lightly but securely. Assume the address position and begin the backswing. Bend the wrists so that as the club reaches hip height its toe points to the sky. Swing the arms down and present the club face squarely to the target at impact. Toward the finish, the toe of the club, at hip height, is again looking to the sky.

FEEL The right wrist bends back on itself and the left rotates a little. At impact the club head seems to lag a little as the back of the left hand looks at the target. You feel a release after impact as the right hand overtakes the left.

BENEFIT Bending your wrists on the back and forward swing establishes the correct alignment of the club face in relation to the swingpath and gives greater ball control.

Hands are opposite torso

Back of left hand, palm of right, and club face are looking at target

Right wrist has overtaken left wrist

Club head lags behind hands, arms, and weight shift to collect ball

81

TENNIS RACKET

PROBLEM Simple movements in golf – such as the action of the hands – often appear complicated and unnatural, leading to uncontrolled shots. Seeing how similar movements are made in other sports can clear up confusion and lead to greater control.

Racket face looks to front at hip height as shoulders turn

Back of left hand looks to front

Weight shifts to right side

DRILL Hold a tennis racket as you would a golf club. Make a backswing as though playing a low forehand return with topspin. At hip height the racket face looks to the front. At impact it looks to the target as your weight shifts to the left. The hands zip the racket over to create topspin so that, at hip height on the forward swing, the face looks to the rear.

FEEL Feel the natural coordination of the arms, hands, and body turning and moving together as you swing the racket through to the finish. Take note of the way the wrists bend to work the racket as the upper body turns on the backswing.

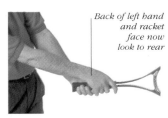

Back of left hand and racket face now look to rear

Right knee folds inward

Back of left hand and racket face both look at target

Weight is firmly on left foot

BENEFIT The hand action in tennis helps clarify the action in golf. It begins with a lag of the club head, then a release at impact as you accelerate to the finish. This creates club head speed and greater ball control.

POINTER DRILL

PROBLEM When you don't bend your wrists correctly in the golf swing you miss the target because the club face is not looking directly toward it at impact.

DRILL Attach a tee temporarily to the face of a long iron. Insert another one into the back of your golf glove so that it sticks out in front. Adopt the address position and check that both tees are pointing to the target. At the start of the backswing move the shoulders, torso, arms, and club away, then begin to bend the wrists. When the club reaches hip height the toe looks to the sky; the tees point to the front. At and through impact the tees point to the target; on the forward swing they point to the rear.

FEEL On the backswing you feel the right wrist bend back on itself as the left one rotates a little. As the left hip clears through impact the wrists release the club face naturally.

Attach tee to club face

At address, both tees point directly to target

BENEFIT The tees act as a simple but effective visual aid for achieving correct wrist action throughout the golf swing. By learning to bend the wrists so that they present the club face square to the target at impact you will send the ball there.

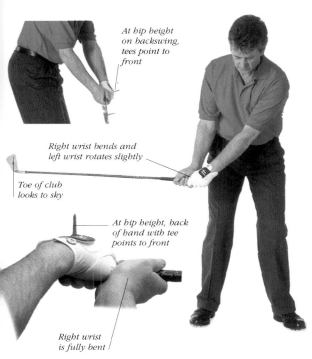

At hip height on backswing, tees point to front

Right wrist bends and left wrist rotates slightly

Toe of club looks to sky

At hip height, back of hand with tee points to front

Right wrist is fully bent

LEFT THUMB UNDER

At top of backswing, wrists are fully cocked and left thumb supports club

Club is on line, with club head square to swingpath

PROBLEM Do you miss the target to the right or left? When the club face is open to its swingpath (looks at the ground) at the top of the backswing, the ball misses on the right; when it is closed (looks at the sky), the ball misses on the left.

DRILL Assume a grip with both palms facing each other. Allow the wrists to bend on the backswing. At the top, check that the left thumb sits under the grip.

Left thumb sits under club grip at top of backswing

FEEL You feel the left thumb supporting the grip and your wrists fully cocked.

BENEFIT At impact you present the club face squarely to the target so that your shots reach the mark.

Club head is square to target

Left thumb is directly under grip

CLOSED CLUB FACE
Club head looks upward;
left thumb is on side of grip.

OPEN CLUB FACE
Club head looks downward;
left thumb is on far side of grip.

SPLIT HANDS

PROBLEM Do you cast the club head from the top of the backswing like a fisherman casts a fly? This results in loss of power, poor balance, and misdirected shots.

DRILL Hold the club so that the right hand is at the end of the grip, with part of it on the shaft. Make a backswing to the top.

Backswing feels wider with split hands grip

Left arm extends and right one folds

Left hand sits in usual position

Right one sits farther down grip

Then let the arms swing down freely. Your feet initiate the downswing by transferring body weight. Your hips rotate to instigate the centrifugal action, which energizes the swing of the arms. The hands and club head follow.

FEEL The weight transfer and the swing of the arms feel as if they happen together, but the weight transfers first. The left hand leads the butt of the grip down to the ball. Feel the width created by an extended left arm.

BENEFIT Club head speed through impact is achieved when movement in the downswing is from feet to hips, arms, and hands. The club head accelerates through the ball, achieving greater distance with less effort.

Right wrist maintains its bend

Club head lags behind weight shift, hip rotation, and swing of arms

SWINGPATH

PROBLEM Do you know that the swingpath of the club head should travel "inside-square-to-inside" of the ball-to-target line but you do not see or feel this? Without an understanding of the geometry, poor shots will prevail.

DRILL Place a club on the ground. This represents the ball-to-target line. Hold another club with both hands, extending your arms forward. Stand square to the club on the ground so that the two clubs appear in line.

    Turn your shoulders as your arms swing up to a half backswing. Keep your eyes on the ground. In your peripheral vision you will see the club shaft track away in an arc. Then let your arms fall freely downward and up again on the other side. The club in your hands brushes with the ball-to-target line on an arc "inside-square-to-inside" of it.

FEEL As the arms fall the club feels as if it is swung outward. As you turn through you feel the arms swinging around and up.

Take up position square to club with arms extended

Clubs look in line with each other

BENEFIT This simple drill helps you establish a sound muscle memory for the essential geometry of the swing. You will improve your swing – and your scores.

Upper body turns to halfway point, with eyes still on ground

Arms swing freely up again on other side

Grip of club points to club on ground

Club head points to club on ground

INSIDE-SQUARE-TO-INSIDE

PROBLEM If you are fearful of hitting the ball to an obstacle to the right you are likely to pull the club from "outside to inside" of the ball-to-target line. Your efforts to steer the ball away from the obstacle result in either a straight pull to the left of the target or a slice into the obstacle on the right.

Club is on line

Club tracks arc low to ground to avoid balls

Shoulders turn fully

DRILL Position a semicircle of balls to represent the arc of swing. Make some shots with the object ball. The semicircle of balls should remain intact after each shot.

FEEL The arms swing freely downward. If you feel your shoulders heave the club down you will scatter the balls.

BENEFIT As long as the club face is at right angles to the target at impact, the ball will fly straight to the target.

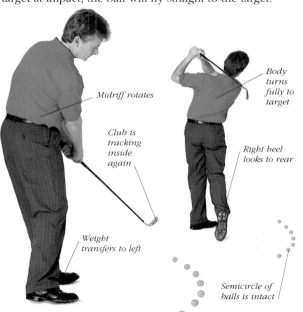

Midriff rotates

Club is tracking inside again

Weight transfers to left

Body turns fully to target

Right heel looks to rear

Semicircle of balls is intact

PLANE OF SWING

PROBLEM Confusion and poor shots arise if your swing action differs according to whether you are using a wood or an iron.

Good posture serves well with both clubs

DRILL Make a backswing with your iron and hold the position at the top. The left hand sits above the right shoulder with the left thumb under the grip. Then swing your driver to the top. The hand position is as before.

FEEL The mechanics of the swing feel the same with both clubs, although you stand more over the ball with the lofted iron.

BENEFIT Although you swing down with an iron and sweep through with a wood, the principles of the swing action are the same for both. This improves your swing action and your whole golf game.

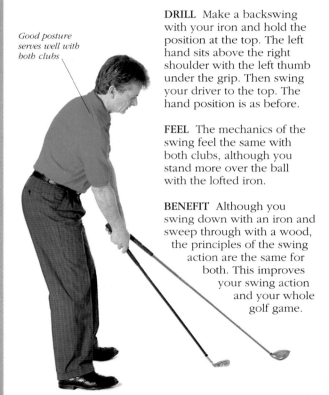

Shaft is on line

Left hand sits above right shoulder

Left hand again sits above right shoulder

Spine angle is slightly more tilted with short iron

Lower body reacts in identical fashion for each club

THE CYLINDER

PROBLEM Does your left shoulder rise up on the backswing? Or does it dip down sharply to the ball? Any change in posture once the swing has begun adversely affects the swingpath and angle of attack of the club face into the ball. This results in errant shots.

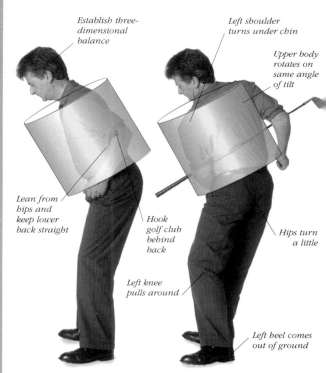

Establish three-dimensional balance

Lean from hips and keep lower back straight

Hook golf club behind back

Left knee pulls around

Left shoulder turns under chin

Upper body rotates on same angle of tilt

Hips turn a little

Left heel comes out of ground

DRILL Hold a club behind your back and lean over from the hips. Make a golf swing by turning first away from and then through to the target without changing the spine's angle of tilt. You will see the grip come around to a point in front of an imaginary ball. Then the club head comes down and around to the same point. Make sure that the shaft angle moves on a constant plane. The spine angle is influenced by the length of the club that you are using.

FEEL On the backswing the left shoulder turns easily under the chin. On the forward swing feel your feet begin to transfer weight. Your hips turn and your right shoulder moves slightly downward and under the chin.

BENEFIT The drill helps you to develop a more consistent swingplane. This leads to better contact with the ball and greater accuracy on all shots.

Right shoulder comes down and under chin

Shaft of club returns on same plane

Hips and midriff turn through to target

Right knee points down target line

Right foot is on toes

BACK TO THE FENCE

Club is on line at top

PROBLEM Do you thin the ball to the right, hit the ground in front of the ball, or hook it to the left? If so, your swingplane is probably too flat – the arms swing the club around the body on the same plane as the turn of the shoulders.

Left hand sits above right shoulder

Line through elbows sits parallel with ground

DRILL Stand about 12 in (30 cm) from a fence, wall, or hedge. At first, reverse the club in your hand as though striking a ball with the grip. Start by making your backswing in slow motion, taking care not to strike the fence as you continue to the top. Bend the wrists when they reach about 8 o'clock. Swing through to the end of the swing, avoiding the fence. Gradually build up your speed.

Club swings through ball and up inside ball-to-target line

FEEL You feel that the arms swing up on a steeper plane than the shoulders. At the start of the action you feel that the shoulders, torso, and arms are turning together.

BENEFIT Your angle of attack becomes more appropriate for the club being used. This drill improves the quality and accuracy of shots.

Hips and midriff rotate to face target

Right knee points down target line

Right heel looks to rear

TWO CLUBS AND MIRROR

PROBLEM Do your shots have no power despite your swing being too fast? You are snatching the club downward too quickly at the start of the swing, killing rhythm, tempo, and timing.

Shoulders, midriff, and arms turn together

DRILL Adopt the golf pose in front of a mirror, holding two clubs. Swing back a little, then through. The hands and arms are not strong enough alone. They require the body to rotate and create a free-flowing swing. Increase the fullness of the swing, seeing how little the arms and hands do.

FEEL The clubs feel lighter the more the body turns. Early weight transfer and midriff rotation on the forward move give a sensation of arms swinging down slowly then the club head accelerating through the foot of the arc.

Midriff and knees rotate

Feet alter weight shift

BENEFIT Although the hands and arms swing the club to strike the ball, the actions of the larger muscles of the legs, midriff, and body fuel and energize the swing action. You will achieve coordinated movement as well as more power.

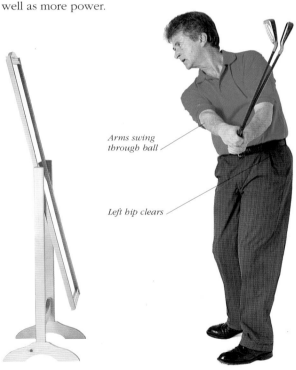

Arms swing through ball

Left hip clears

BACK TO FRONT

PROBLEM Are you so focused on your backswing that you forget to swing the club through the ball? If so, you hit "at" it rather than "past" it. This results in a loss of distance and accuracy.

DRILL Go straight to the finish of the golf swing. Hold it. Notice how your body feels. Then let the arms fall down-ward and up into the top of the backswing, turning to accommodate it. Once the club has arrived, swing through to the finish again. Repeat this, holding the finish in a relaxed and balanced way as though posing for the camera.

FEEL You are more aware of the two turns of the body and of the weight transfer. You feel the club accelerate through the imaginary ball to the finish.

Hands sit over left shoulder

Torso points to left of target

Hips look to target, in line with midriff and right knee

Feet are in line with left knee, hips, and shoulders

Arms fall freely downward

Left thumb sits under grip

Shoulders turn fully so back faces target

Hips turn slightly with left hip coming around

Left heel comes out of ground slightly

BENEFIT Your backswing feels more natural and you are more focused on reaching and holding the end of the swing position. This promotes increased speed through impact and leads to more distance.

CLUB HEAD AWARENESS

PROBLEM The club is seldom where it should be during the golf swing. If you have no awareness of the club head arriving at the end of the backswing, you will have no feeling of rhythm, tempo, or timing for what is to follow.

DRILL Reverse the club so that you are holding the shaft just below the club head. Assume your address position as usual. Swing the club in a smooth, rhythmical way from a full backswing to a complete finish. Then make further swings, holding it the right way around.

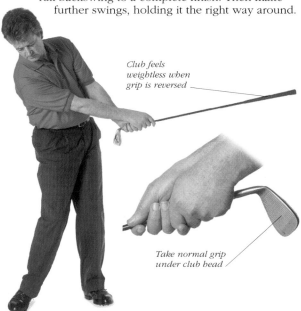

Club feels weightless when grip is reversed

Take normal grip under club head

FEEL The reversed club gives a feeling of weightlessness. When you swing with the club the right way around it becomes easy to tell where the club head is because you feel its weight. You are immediately aware of the precise moment when the club head arrives at the end of the backswing, and you can feel it swish through the ball.

BENEFIT Making a few swings this way at the start of a practice session or a round of golf quickly heightens your awareness of rhythm, tempo, and timing.

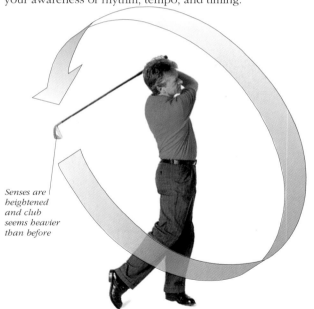

Senses are heightened and club seems heavier than before

FREE FALL

PROBLEM Do you have difficulty transferring your weight at the start of the forward swing? Does your swing seem to take a lot of effort yet produce little power? If so, you are probably pulling the club downward with your shoulders as though splitting logs.

DRILL Swing the club to the top of the backswing. Then, keeping the shoulders fully turned, allow the arms to fall freely downward at the same time as your body weight shifts to the left side. The hands separate from the right shoulder as they fall to hip height. Repeat this many times in front of a mirror. Notice how the left arm remains comfortably extended and how the wrists maintain their angle as the butt of the grip falls downward.

Hands are above right shoulder

Turn into right side

Body weight balances on right foot

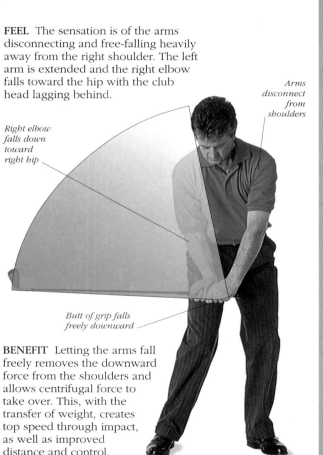

FEEL The sensation is of the arms disconnecting and free-falling heavily away from the right shoulder. The left arm is extended and the right elbow falls toward the hip with the club head lagging behind.

Arms disconnect from shoulders

Right elbow falls down toward right hip

Butt of grip falls freely downward

BENEFIT Letting the arms fall freely removes the downward force from the shoulders and allows centrifugal force to take over. This, with the transfer of weight, creates top speed through impact, as well as improved distance and control.

HIP IT

PROBLEM No matter
how hard you try, your
friends keep knocking
the ball farther than
you. Your hands and
arms are probably
doing all the work
and cannot
generate the
necessary
club head
speed through
the ball to
achieve great
distance.

*Wrists bend to
point shaft of
club to sky*

*Shoulders
and torso
turn away
from target*

*Arms swing up
to half backswing*

*Body weight
moves to right side*

DRILL Swing the club to a half
backswing. Disconnect the
arms from the shoulders,
letting them fall downward
with the butt of the club
leading the way. Generate
power by "hitting the ball with
your hips." Use a No. 6 or 7
iron at first, to send the ball
about 100 yds (100 m). Then
use other clubs similarly.

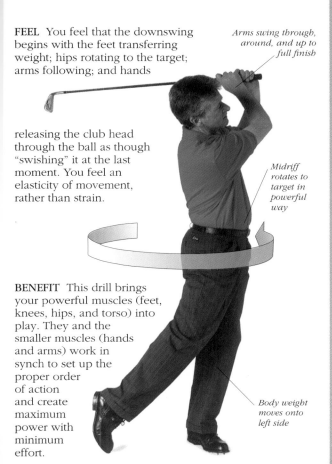

FEEL You feel that the downswing begins with the feet transferring weight; hips rotating to the target; arms following; and hands

releasing the club head through the ball as though "swishing" it at the last moment. You feel an elasticity of movement, rather than strain.

BENEFIT This drill brings your powerful muscles (feet, knees, hips, and torso) into play. They and the smaller muscles (hands and arms) work in synch to set up the proper order of action and create maximum power with minimum effort.

Arms swing through, around, and up to full finish

Midriff rotates to target in powerful way

Body weight moves onto left side

BALL UNDER RIGHT FOOT

PROBLEM Are your shots sometimes pulled to the left, and other times to the right? Do you lose your balance on every full swing, with your right knee moving outside your right foot on the backswing, creating a sway and reverse pivot? If so, you have forgotten that the golf swing must be contained within the width of your stance.

DRILL Take up your stance as though playing a shot. Place a ball or a small wedge under your right foot. Make a few swings. The restriction imposed by the ball under your foot prevents the right knee from moving laterally.

FEEL Your first impression is of confinement. Your lower body wants to move laterally but cannot. At the top you are balanced and ready to drive your weight through the ball. The throughswing feels more compact yet automatic.

RIGHT KNEE SWAY
Right knee is bent and has moved laterally outside foot.

WEIGHT SHIFT
Weight shifts to outside edge of foot and balance is lost.

BENEFIT This drill makes your upper body better able to turn over the right foot on the backswing in the appropriate coiling action. This sets up the correct order of movement on the forward swing. The result is that your golf swing is a more powerful unit because it is better balanced throughout. The timing becomes more naturally coordinated. More consistent play ensues.

Shoulders turn fully over right foot

Hips turn a little

Balance points of shoulders, right hip, knee, and foot support each other

Wedge golf ball under your right foot

Balance has shifted into right side and remains within feet

111

ADDRESS/IMPACT POSITION

PROBLEM Have you been told to return to the address position at impact? This breaks down the proper order of movement of the forward swing, promoting overactive hand and arm action, and underactive foot and leg work. "Hooks," "blocks," and other inconsistent shots result.

Balance points of shoulders, hips, knees, and feet support each other

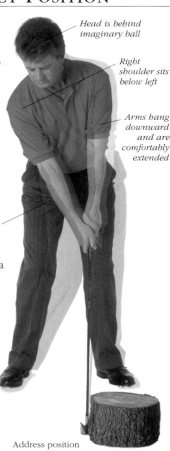

Head is behind imaginary ball

Right shoulder sits below left

Arms hang downward and are comfortably extended

DRILL Set up with your club head resting against a log, tree, stone, or other immovable object. At this point you are simply standing as though ready for action. Then make as though to move the object forward from this standing position. To do so with your hands and arms alone is too much of a strain. Causing the object to move requires input from the big muscles too.

12   Address position

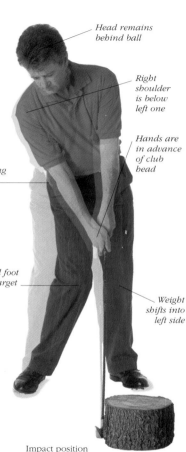

FEEL When you try to move the object, the body weight is firmly on the left foot; the hips are clearing; the left arm and large deltoid muscles around the left side are energized.

Head remains behind ball

Right shoulder is below left one

Hands are in advance of club head

Hips and midriff are clearing and generating centrifugal power

Right knee and foot drive toward target

Weight shifts into left side

BENEFIT You will realize that, just as a karate expert focuses on a point beyond the object and passes his fist through the object, a more powerful golf shot results when you swing through the ball, not to it.

Impact position

113

BUNKER DRILLS

Do not be intimidated by the bunker shot: it is easy when you follow basic principles. This is one of the few shots in golf in which the ball and the club face do not meet. The ball flies off a cushion of sand rather than off the face of the club. The purpose of the swing is to accelerate the club face through the sand in front of and beneath the ball, maintaining maximum loft on the face.

For open club face, take conventional hold but with scorelines on club face looking to right

Align body to left of target

Club face is open and looks to target

Position ball slightly left of center

Align shoulders, hips, knees, and feet to left

The right hand and wrist bend early in the takeaway and remain bent through the impact zone. This action makes the ball pop up so that it lands softly on the green. Always swing through the sand to a complete finish whenever possible.

Club face looks directly at target

Different lies require special strategies (see page 118). These pages show the set-up for a conventional "splash" shot.

Swing club along line of stance, across ball-to-target line

115

TEE DRILL

PROBLEM Does the fear of hitting the ball too far make you lose heart? Does your weight end up on the back foot as you attempt to scoop out the ball with a flick of the club head and wrists? Do you find bunker shots difficult for this reason? If so, you have forgotten the basic bunker principle that a fully lofted club face must accelerate through the sand beneath the ball.

Sink tee below surface and place ball on top

Wrists bend early in takeaway as arms swing up

Shoulders turn fully

Body weight favors left side

Body is perfectly balanced

Align stance slightly to left of target

Make club face open to grip

Ball is nearer left foot

116

DRILL Push a tee into the sand and place a ball on top. Adopt the usual grip and stance, with the ball slightly to the left of center. Make a swing, aiming to dislodge the tee and hit it – not the ball – onto the green. Keep the right wrist bent backward as the club enters the sand.

FEEL Your swing feels much longer through the sand. Your hips clear out of the way to enable your arms to swing freely as they lead the club head through the sand.

BENEFIT You develop a smoother swing action. The ball floats high and lands on the green.

Focus on dislodging tee

Hips clear

Arms lead club face down and through sand beneath ball

117

PLUGGED BALL

PROBLEM When faced with a plugged ball, do you panic and your movements become erratic?

DRILL Stand square to the ball-to-target line, with the club face aligned to target and your body weight on the left side. Position the ball back in the stance. Bend the wrists early as you turn the shoulders, then release them early in the downswing. Aim to get the club face into the sand behind the ball on a steep angle of attack.

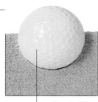

Ball is half-buried in sand

Align body square to target with weight on left side

Right wrist bends at beginning of backswing

Place ball opposite right foot with club face square

Settle feet into sand

118

Hands release club head like fisherman casting a fly

FEEL The hands and arms feel that they are doing most of the work. Feel the right wrist bend back on itself as you begin the backswing. Then feel both hands roll the club face through sand and ball.

BENEFIT This simple technique gives you the confidence and skill to get your plugged ball onto the green.

Hands and arms do the work

Right hand rolls over left one

Toe of club overtakes heel

PLAN B

PLAN B

PROBLEM Are you still trying to scoop the club head under the ball with the right hand in an attempt to dig it out, rather than let the club head lag into the sand? When all other methods have failed, try this one.

DRILL Stand square but with the ball slightly to left of center. Grip the club as usual with the left hand but, with the right, hold it in the fingertips and wrap the hand over so that all four knuckles are showing.

Make your swing, letting the wrists bend.

Hold club in tips of fingers

Position right hand so that all four knuckles are showing

Weight is on left side

Stand square to target

Ball is slightly to left of center

Wrap right hand around grip so all knuckles show

120

Left wrist is cupped at top of backswing

As your weight moves into the left side, swish the club head into and through the sand.

FEEL As the wrists bend, the club face seems to open greatly. The left wrist is cupped and the right palm points down at the top of the backswing.

BENEFIT The strength of the right hand is diffused, and the left arm and hand are free to lag the club face into the sand. The ball pops up and lands on the green.

Wrists swish club head into and through sand

ONGOING
PRACTICE

*The third step to becoming a good
golfer is to believe in yourself and
your ability, and to know how to
maximize your strengths.*

HOW TO BELIEVE IN YOURSELF

Hints on using drills and on how to practice have been given on pages 14–18. There is one more vital task to perform on a regular basis before the benefits of your endeavors become evident in your game – you must practice belief in yourself.

○ The subconscious mind is a silent computer that translates every thought into action. "You are what you think you are," is an old saying that rings true on the golf course.

○ Use your imagination to "see" a successful end result. Believe that the drills that you have worked on will greatly improve your game.

○ Believe that your game is progressing.

○ Imagine yourself playing each golf shot easily from now on, without the need for too much conscious thought or effort.

○ Avoid using willpower to play well: this suggests that you can't play well without it.

○ Your subconscious does not react to willful commands – it responds only to your faith and belief in the outcome.

○ As you practice your new skills, affirm to yourself early and often how much clearer you are in your mind; how you can feel yourself progressing; how much better you feel about yourself as a golfer. Your behavior changes, as does your mood. You find yourself doing the right things without having to think about them. Suddenly things begin to work out for you.

○ When you have a feeling of success, you will have success.

○ Simply know that you are now a better player.

○ Do not underestimate the power of this affirmative mental process.

SELF-AFFIRMATION
*A good golfing technique
needs to be supported by
a firm belief in yourself
in order to make you
perform well on the
golf course.*

How to Lower your Scores

A positive mental attitude, as well as technical skill, is required when playing golf. All expert players use their sense of reasoning on the golf course. Here are some ways to keep your mind focused when competing:

o It is impossible to hit good shots on the golf course if you are thinking about your technique. Play golf – negotiate the ball from A to B in the most economical way possible. Save working on your technique for the practice green.

o Give every hole a plan and every shot a realistic target. Make your targets big ones – they are easier to hit and give you confidence.

o Never compare yourself with any other player – you are a unique golfer, with your own style, strengths, experience, and par. Keep to your game plan within these parameters.

o Always play the course – never your opponent – for the same reasons.

o Play to your strengths, using the clubs that work best for you, whenever possible. Save working on your weaknesses until you are off the course.

o Utilize the teeing area to suit your shape of shot. If, for example, your drives normally set off to the left before bending to the right, tee off from the right side of the teeing area, making your landing area bigger.

o Keep in the present tense by dealing with each shot honestly and leaving the next shot until later. You cannot hit a good shot if you are preoccupied with the next one.

o Don't count your score until the end and avoid the "all I have to do" syndrome.

o Be patient – particularly with yourself. No player hits bad shots on purpose – accidents happen even to the best player.

TACTICAL PLAY
*Once you have
mastered golfing
techniques, learn
to play tactically
on the golf course
so that you can
maximize your
strengths.*

GLOSSARY

ball-to-target line The imaginary line between the ball and the target.

block A shot that sets off to the right of the target, caused by a lateral slide.

closed club face Club face is aligned to the left of its swingpath.

closed stance Body is aligned to the right of the target line.

draw A mild right-to-left flight of the ball.

fade A mild left-to-right flight of the ball.

hook A ball that sets off to the right of target but bends severely to the left in flight.

inside-square-to-inside The arc of swing that brushes with, and remains on the near side of, the ball-to-target line.

muscle memory The ability to repeat a movement automatically, without conscious thought.

object ball The ball to be played when, in practice, other balls act as decoys.

off line When the ball or the club face is pulled off the intended line of flight.

on line When the ball or the club face is direct to target.

open club face Club face is aligned to the right of its swingpath.

open stance Body is aligned to the left of the target line.

reverse pivot When the body weight remains on the left foot at the top of the backswing instead of moving to the right.

sweetspot The area of the club face – usually the center – that produces the perfect flight or roll.

thin To strike the ball by the bottom edge of the blade, usually on the upswing, causing it to shoot along the ground, out of control.

ACKNOWLEDGMENTS

Thanks to Mark Tattam for his design assistance.
The author is indebted to the Tommy Armour Golf Co. (Scotland) Ltd. for their support in providing equipment and Mark Scot golf shirts.